G Loves You Immensely

GOD Loves You Immensely

Chiara Lubich

Compiled by
Caterina Ruggiu and Michel Vandeleene

Translated by William Hartnett

NEW CITY PRESS
www.newcitypress.com

Published in the United States by New City Press
202 Comforter Blvd., Hyde Park, NY 12538
www.newcitypress.com
©2010 New City Press (English translation)

Translated by William Hartnett from the original Italian
Dio ti ama immensamente
©2009 Città Nuova Editrice, Rome, Italy

Cover design by Leandro de Leon

Biblical citations are taken from:
The New Jerusalem Bible
©1985 Doubleday a Division of Bantam
Doubleday Dell Publishing Group, Inc.,
New York, NY 10103, except where indicated (*)
in which case they are our own translation.

Library of Congress Cataloging-in-Publication Data:

Lubich, Chiara, 1920-2008.
  [Dio ti ama immensamente. English]
  God loves you immensely / Chiara Lubich ; compiled by Caterina Ruggiu and Michel Vandeleene ; translated by William Hartnett.
       p. cm.
  Includes bibliographical references.
  ISBN 978-1-56548-339-2 (pbk. : alk. paper) 1. God (Christianity)—Love. 2. Spirituality—Catholic Church. I. Ruggiu, Caterina. II. Vandeleene, Michel. III. Title.
  BT140.L7913 2010
  242'.722—dc22
                                                                            2009039946

Printed in the United States of America

Contents

Introduction 7

I Would Tell You of God's Love 11

Notes 67

For Further Reading 71

Introduction

These pages are good news in every sense of the word, from forgetting the worries of the day (Peter invited us to cast our worries on God, *"because he cares for you,"* 1 Pt 5:7) to the certainty that God loves each and every one and demonstrated this by giving his life (*"For even the Son of Man did not come to be served, but to serve, and to give his life as a ransom for many,"* Mk 10:45*). For every sentence in this book you can find a corresponding passage in the Bible, the authoritative source of all Chiara's thinking.

The new point of view through which the young Chiara looks at various issues is also linked to the context in which she expresses her ideas. She is writing during World War II. Often we can imagine the sound of the bombs falling behind Chiara's words, the call to renewal and the response of faith to so much meaningless pain. The repeated hints of death are not a sign of pessimism or of giving in to sadness, but are part of the normal daily events in the midst of war. Chiara's words are always an invitation to live the present moment to the fullest by keeping focused on what is truly worthwhile. Then suffering reveals its positive and constructive mission; that is, not only to accept pain, but to see it as an opportunity to share in the suffering that Jesus went through out of love for us on the cross. Chiara's language soars when she shares Jesus forsaken with her readers (cf. Mt 27:46; Mk 15:34). Here is a god who, driven by love, *forgets* that he is God. He enters into oblivion, losing himself in the one he loves to the point of no longer remembering who he is.

Chiara destroys the idea of a vengeful and judgmental God and reveals the God who is Love. But Love needs to be loved and from a very early age, this becomes her mission. Understood in light of this divine love, her appeals to love Love, to abandon ourselves to God without reserve, to spare nothing for ourselves, are all to be understood within the light of this divine love. For this reason Chiara writes that God alone matters — not because the things in human life are not good, but because they only find their rightful place, their reason for being, in God.

This does not mean that we should become hermits, or give up all human affection. Chiara is expressing a deeper need: that of restoring God to his place, the place he deserves in the ranking of our emotions, to render every love divine, eternal, stable, and true by referring them all to our love for God. She writes: "When our inmost being belongs to God, everything else will have value." It's a question of prioritizing while never annihilating what is earthly and human. Chiara is inviting us to rethink everything in the light of her luminous discovery that God is Love.

It's an arduous task, indeed, and Chiara herself is the first to recognize this: "I fall," she admits. And with these simple words she reassures all those who feel they will never make it. This is perhaps the most incisive message that emerges from the pages of this book: What matters is not that we are already perfect, but that we are always trying again and again, loving and living for others. Chiara is the first to start, she shares in the effort with us, demonstrating to us that holiness, that ambitious but necessary aim, is truly within the reach of all.

Collections of quotations from famous people are in circulation everywhere. Often these brief sentences offer rich aphorisms that are able to strike at the heart of many issues. Chiara Lubich's words had never been put together in such a format, a gap that this small book seeks to overcome. These helpful sentences express what we ourselves sometimes think and experience but can never quite seem to put into words so well. They can help us to live what we feel inside to be our true destiny.

Maria Chiara Janner

Editorial Note: In choosing how to capitalize pronouns which refer to God, the translator followed the choice of the author.

I Would Tell You
of God's Love

How I would wish to have you near
    to me now
and to talk to you and talk to you.
I would tell you of the greatness of God's
    love.
I would speak words to you
that before I didn't know
and was only able to just barely make out,
but that now I know well.[1]

∼

May God draw you
with words
that only the love of a God
can say.[2]

∼

Perhaps you didn't always
think that you were so precious a thing,
the very object of God's love.
But He loved you,
even before you were born,
and soon you will be returning to Him.[3]

𝒜rise to a totally new life:
believe that God loves you.
I assure you the fullness of joy here below.⁴

~

"*My God, my All!*"
Let these words spoken by Francis of Assisi
in prayer
be true for your heart,
most especially your heart,
for the heart is where our being lies.⁵

~

𝒜lso for you
the Most High
has marked out
a plan of love.⁶

Re-enter into yourself:
search for God,
your God,
the one who lives in you![7]

~

God doesn't want many things from you
except your heart.
Give it to Him
and you will have given everything!
It's so easy to satisfy Him![8]

~

In God we can do all things.
Even the most daring flights
are reserved for hearts
that live by faith in a god
who is God, Love, Omnipotent.[9]

A neighbor passes near to us in each
   moment!
It's Jesus.
Measure your love for God
by the love that you bring to that
   neighbor.[10]

∼

"Let us love in deeds and in truth"
   (JN 3:18*).
Not: "Let us do deeds" and "Let us
   speak the truth."
No, "Let us love...."
Love is what counts.[11]

∼

Only Love
makes us brothers and sisters.[12]

Many
discuss,
talk,
correct,
and write for others to read.
Few
LIVE.[13]

~

Always get up again.
Even if you have to get up
a million times
every day.[14]

~

What good would it do Him to be
   infinitely merciful?
What good would it do Him,
if it were not for our sins?[15]

God will be everything for you
in just a few years,
as soon as this brief life passes by!
Throw yourself onto Him![16]

~

Just think:
we can love God
with this tiny heart!
We can love God!
No one will take away this love from us,
not even the most terrific bombardment.[17]

~

Love?
You want it?
God is Love.[18]

Don't let your youth escape you,
and amid the sobs of a life in ruin
you will have to repeat the words
   of St. Augustine:
"Late have I loved You!"[19]

∼

Look at the stars,
the life that is in everything
and feel God.
Plunge yourself into Him![20]

∼

Just think:
God came to earth only once
and that once as a man,
and he let himself be hung on a cross![21]

God allows moments of darkness,
of agitation,
and bitterness,
so that we might know what we are
and, conscious of our misery,
and of our nothingness,
we might throw ourselves back onto Him,
with total trust,
only in Him.[22]

∼

If your life has proven wearisome till now
perhaps the time has arrived for you
to take a stand:
with Him or against Him.[23]

You mustn't give things to the Lord
with a long face
or closed heart.
He "loves a cheerful giver"
   (2 COR 9:7*).[24]

～

God's mercy
prospers at a cost to us!
We give him our rags
which he will burn
and make use of for something good.[25]

～

"Even the hairs of your head are
   counted" (MT 10:30).
We have a need to feel watched over and
   loved by God.[26]

As much mercy
as we show to others
will be shown to us.
No more.[27]

~

People alone with themselves
are always bored
because in themselves
they find nothingness.
Jesus is Love,
Fullness,
Joy,
Peace,
Richness!
And if our soul
isn't *one* with Him
it's nothing but an emptiness.[28]

There is only one thing you must do:
be one with God
and, when you are,
you will be one with everyone.[29]

≈

The Lord dwells in the depth of your
   soul.
Be worthy of Him![30]

≈

Throw your every anxiety on Him
who calms storms
and strengthens hearts.[31]

≈

Do you know Jesus forsaken?
Do you know that He's given us
   everything?
What more could a god give to us
out of love
than to forget that He is God?[32]

Those who love
can also fear suffering.
Look at Peter the apostle
who kept far from the cross.
But those who know they are loved,
cannot be frightened.
St. John was like this,
the youngest,
the most loved,
the only one who ran to the foot
　of the cross.[33]

Faith in Love is precisely what you are
　lacking.
Don't you know that He cares for the
　little birds and the lilies of the field?
How much more dear to Him must you
　be!
How much more dear![34]

Lose that burden that's
  weighing you down
and keeping you from flying.[35]

∿

God who is Love can only see with the
  Heart.[36]

∿

Jesus who is our model
taught us just two things
that are one:
to be children
of a single Father
and brothers and sisters
of each other.[37]

∿

The Gospel
is a personal gift
of God's love
for each one of us.[38]

Since God is Love, He is Trinity.[39]

~

Never desire perfection.
Desire to love Him;
and love Him,
moment by moment,
accomplishing
the divine will
with all your heart,
with all your mind,
with all your strength.[40]

~

Look around you.
Everything in the world passes away.
Each day evening comes,
and evening drops so quickly.
Every life has a sunset
that quickly falls,
yours too![41]

Run into the world and sing to Love![42]

≈

Have God
as the only object of the affection in your heart,
as the only Father,
brother,
friend,
consoler,
doctor,
medicine,
spouse of your soul.
And, like the child
resting on its mother,
don't rest on anything but Him.[43]

≈

May Love make you appreciate
how much he loved you
and how much he loves you![44]

It is God's command
that we love Him with all our heart;
that is, that we do the will of God with
    all our heart,
which is right now to love each other
and to love the neighbor who is at our side
moment by moment,
to such a point and with such momentum
that our neighbor will be swept away by
    our Ideal
and constrained
by love
to love God with his whole heart.[45]

∾

Mary is a creature
who freely
made God her All
and by Him
was made
Mother of God.[46]

Forget everything in life:
office, work, responsibility,
hunger, thirst, rest,
even your very own soul,
so that you possess only Him!
There! Now you have everything![47]

~

Only love Love![48]

~

Place yourself at the service
of God's plans.[49]

~

Will you be faithful
to the One
working in you?[50]

I know: you'll fall.
I also fall, often, always.
But when I lift my gaze to Him
and see Him there, incapable of revenge,
since He is nailed to a cross because of
   His boundless love,
I let myself be caressed,
by His infinite mercy
and I know
it's the only thing
that must win out in me.[51]

~

Even from the evil that we commit
(the only thing that is truly ours)
God can draw a greater good
than the good the evil had taken away.[52]

There's not a suffering in the world,
a joy in the world,
a feeling in the world
that we cannot drown
in the love of God![53]

∾

You need to lose everything
in order to find it again in the All![54]

∾

Love the Crucified!
That's where it all lies,
all the love of a God.
He couldn't have given us more.[55]

∾

Our faith that He loves us
will provide us with
the greatest success.[56]

Welcome
all the opportunities
that God gives you
to do
your part.[57]

∼

If love dominates in people's hearts,
in the hearts of all the people on the planet,
then God cannot but make his voice
heard
and his truth in the depths of their spirit.[58]

∼

It's sufficient that just one
be what she should be,
for others to be what they should be.[59]

∼

Don't be one of those so-called
 Christians
who draw hatred to Christ
because they bear only His name.[60]

Jesus ran with giant strides,
because He had to reclaim
his Father's glory.[61]

~

No more worrying about the future:
Jesus doesn't want it.
If you want to worry,
He will leave you be.
But if you leave everything to his love,
He will be the one to worry about you
in a wonderful way.[62]

~

Give your weaknesses to Him!
He will give you
the flame of *love of God!*[63]

When you are misunderstood,
when they fight against you,
and you are seen as evil,
covered in shame,
hold for certain
that Jesus is with you
and that He is giving
an authentic sign
that you are his disciple:
the cross.[64]

~

Believe it:
God is in you![65]

~

Your battle cry:
"Because I love You!"[66]

~

I would like to run through the world
to gather hearts for God
and I feel that all the hearts in the world
will never be enough for a love as great as
   He![67]

The way of love
is a joy that the sun never sets on,
a joy born
from the awareness
of being with
the One we love![68]

∼

Your tiny heart
is a mystery of the love of God.
It sings only when
it is loved by an infinite Love
and when it can love
an infinite Love.[69]

∼

Burst through every dam,
every shadow,
every difficulty,
every narrow thought
and keep your eye on the Heaven
that is there waiting for us.[70]

In this life
that runs by like a flash,
one thing remains true,
and that one thing we should ask of God:
to love him.[71]

∼

We give up
a small thing,
and He gives back
the full measure of His immense love.[72]

∼

It seems to me
that God has torn open the heavens
with a cry:
"You are my children whom I love!"[73]

∼

We feel
neither poor nor alone on this earth,
because we have discovered
our relationship with God.[74]

God is with those who suffer.[75]

~

Let God reign in your hearts!
Let Him work!
Do not stand in the way
of His action.[76]

~

Whoever is in the arms of God
who is Love,
must be without worry and doubt,
because every concern,
every disturbance
is from the Evil One, from the devil.[77]

~

Chase away the scruples.
Don't you believe that Jesus can forgive you
after He was abandoned for you
on the cross?[78]

The only thing
that really draws down
blessings from on high
and the love of God,
is charity.[79]

~

To love God means
to love each other
with practical (effective) love
and gentle (affective) love.[80]

~

I have seen first hand
that God among us accomplishes the impossible:
the miraculous![81]

~

For God it is enough
that our hearts are willing to be set ablaze
with love for Him.[82]

When you're down,
burdened by your humanity,
abandon yourself to God.
Give yourself to Him.
He'll take care of things.[83]

～

God is in the tabernacle.
There is where He is waiting for you!
There is where He is calling you to.[84]

～

Go ahead, study and work.
But let your heart be *always* with Him.[85]

～

Love the One
who in the evening of your life
will look only at your tiny heart.
You'll be alone with Him at that moment;
terribly unhappy will be the one whose
    heart is filled with vanity,
wonderfully happy the one whose heart is full
of the infinite Love of God![86]

Let us feel
that we are at the service of God,
forever under the loving command of a Father,
who commands
only to bring about in us his plan
which is our happiness.[87]

∼

I would like to cry out to the whole world:
put every worry in God's hands,
He will take care of it.[88]

∼

Where there is Jesus
danger flees
and obstacles vanish.
He vanquishes them because
he is Love![89]

How unclever of Christians
not to take advantage of the little bit of sludge
they have in their hearts!
Mercy would have nothing to do
if it were not for those
who keep it working
with their weaknesses![90]

∽

I would like to go to my tomb as He did,
with just one thought in my mind:
"Consummatum est" (JN 19:30*).
It is accomplished.
I could not have loved more here on earth.[91]

∽

Everything passes away
and what remains
is only the amount
of God's love
that we gather in our hearts.[92]

Get up! Take courage!
Don't object to difficulties.
Be a child,
and God will be your Father,
and He will lead you
by the hand.[93]

~

Believe that God loves you,
for when it came to you He didn't spare
    anything.[94]

~

We have only one Father:
the one who is in Heaven.
Only one Mother:
The Virgin, Mother of Love.
Only one Brother:
Jesus
by whom we are all brothers
and have the same spirit.[95]

Whether we suffer
or whether we rejoice,
we always believe
that God loves us
immensely.[96]

≈

Whether you love the Infinite Love
 who is God, I don't know.
I only hope
and wish that you do,
for your own happiness.[97]

≈

Let us not allow anything painful to
 pass by us in life
without accepting it
and desiring it
in order to prove to God
who is immense Love,
our own small
but tenacious
love![98]

What pay
will God ever give
to someone who has given
all his life to Him,
dedicating it totally
to the coming of his Reign!
I think the pay will be enormous!

God is always lavish in His giving![99]

~

Let us allow God to act.
Let us not impede his omnipotence
with the meanness of our views.[100]

~

God loves our weaknesses;
we are His little creations.[101]

~

A person is love
if he or she is nothingness
filled with God.[102]

If you want to run
along God's way
expand your heart
with mercy![103]

∽

The important thing
is starting again,
knowing how to begin again.
It's humble.
It's love.[104]

∽

Holiness is not "optional."
It is "obligatory."[105]

∽

Break any tie
that binds you to thoughts of the
"world" and feel your heart beating
with only one affection,
wide as creation and beyond it,
God, your Father![106]

Don't let a moment go by
without being
one with Love.[107]

~

God works with good
and with adverse circumstances
to make you fall into his Light,
into his infinite Love.[108]

~

Whoever is a child of the heavenly
   Father
who is always on guard to protect us,
never doubts
but is only confident — in his love alone.[109]

~

I have to, I want to make him loved
   by the whole world,
because He was left crucified and abandoned
for me.[110]

We have only one faith
now that Christ has brought us the good
   news:
we believe in God who is Love;
who created us out of love;
who has redeemed us out of love;
who wants to save us out of love;
who asks for our love
in order to give us himself
who is Love.[111]

∽

Remember
that God's judgment
will be a test on love.[112]

∽

Satisfy your thirst for Him,
which torments you under many forms
perhaps unbeknown to you,
by contemplating Him
the beautiful and serene
Lord of Heaven and earth.[113]

Everything is God's.
Give everything to God
and you will be acting according to justice.
Give your whole being —
heart, mind, will, physical strength,
    property;
what you are, and what you have.
Give it all to God.
It is just.
First of all give your heart,
because God is Love and He wants love.
And wherever your heart is, there is your
    entire being.[114]

∼

When our inmost self
is God's,
everything else has value.[115]

∼

Never forsake the Love
that lives in your heart.[116]

You will find again only what you've
given,
not what you've saved.[117]

~

Time is a flash
and, in our hands,
it is only a fleeting moment.[118]

~

If you succeeded to have mercy in
your heart
you would have everything.[119]

~

Loving is the life of God.
It must also be ours.[120]

If Jesus came upon earth,
if he was made man,
if there is a deep yearning in his
divine and human heart,
it is only this:
to be the Savior,
to be the doctor!
He wants nothing else.[121]

~

To be Christ
you have to be like him:
a savior, a merciful one.
Because Christ did not come
to "make an appearance,"
but to fix what was broken,
to save what had been lost,
to love and to draw to himself
those who were detached.[122]

To live Jesus
it is necessary to live
under the direction
of the Holy Spirit.[123]

∼

Love God
and open your arms out to everyone
to make of them all many brothers and sisters
and to place in each one a spark of divine love.[124]

∼

Everything was given to us by God
out of love:
everything must return to God out of love.[125]

∼

We are fragile earthen vessels:
if we don't have confidence in God
we soon begin to stumble and fall down.[126]

What matters in life?
To love You matters.[127]

Up and onward!
Every day takes care of itself
and not of tomorrow.[128]

God is Love.
And God will judge
first and above all
the interior, the intimate recesses
of your heart.[129]

My one and only desire,
my passion,
is that Love be loved.[130]

Why are we afraid to say to everyone
that here below we are only passing
   through
and that there above we will be staying
   forever?[131]

∼

God alone is Everything!
All else is vanity.[132]

∼

God loves
as God.[133]

∼

God is Love!
And suffering is the tough test of Love,
its unmistakably divine seal.[134]

∼

What a future there will be for us
if we take the total risk
of giving ourselves to Him
without *ever* turning back on the offer![135]

To be pure
we shouldn't deprive the heart
or repress love.
We need to expand the heart
to the measure of the heart of Jesus
and to love everyone.[136]

∾

Be there where God has put you.
Be there out of love.[137]

∾

"Cast every anxiety on him
because he cares for you" (1 Pt 5:7*).
"*Every,*" including yours.
Jesus will take care of it.
If you worry,
it means that you don't trust Him.
When we know that something has been
put in good hands,
we no longer worry about it.
Continuing to worry would be an offense
against the person
to whom we had entrusted the thing.[138]

Having a simple eye = one vision of things:
seeing only *one* Father;
only *one* God in our neighbor;
having only *one* brother:
Jesus.[139]

~

Love each other
and you will have done everything.[140]

~

Enjoy your unity,
but for God
and not for yourself.
Catherine of Siena admonishes us
to love God for God,
our neighbor for God,
oneself for God,
never for ourselves.
Our unity too
should be loved for God![141]

Instead of always looking at your soul,
why don't you look at His thirst
to consume,
and to wipe away
miseries?[142]

~

I always pay for the light
and the love that God gives me
with my miseries.
And for this reason
I always have enough for others too.[143]

~

A merciful heart has a divine flavor to it.[144]

~

Christ cries out on the cross:
"My God, my God why have you
    abandoned me?" (MK 15:34).
And He is God!
Even though He cries out.
Precisely because He cries out:
the Beautiful God of Love
who gives the world
a great gift, a gift as great as God![145]

When God works
(and He works if we let Him),
He works miracles.[146]

~

Jesus has a supreme need
to exercise mercy.
Make Him happy
and whenever you feel weighed down by
    your miseries,
give them to Him.
He wants nothing else
but to wipe away miseries.[147]

~

Always forgive,
just forgive.[148]

~

We start the work from here.
We will continue it from there above
through the people who will follow us.[149]

There are many beautiful things on
    earth!
God is the more beautiful![150]

~

If in a few words
I could say the reason for my life,
those words would be:
"I love God
and I would like to love Him
as He was never loved before.
I labor to make Him be loved."[151]

~

The world
isn't so much in need of new laws and
    new rules.
It's in need of people
who can bring order to the love,
the charity that lies deep within
    themselves.
This order is justice.
And it is only from this order
that laws will have value.[152]

In our thinking
and in the feelings of our hearts,
may we always go beyond
all the limits that human life sets up
    before us,
and constantly tend,
through force of habit,
towards universal brotherhood
in one Father:
God.[153]

∼

Jesus knew
that the Most Holy Trinity
was eternal bliss
and came down as the God Man,
to redeem humankind,
wanting to draw along
all those He loved
into the comm-Unity of the Three.[154]

Jesus came among us
wanting to leave his fragrance with us,
his ambiance,
making the earth
into Heaven's antechamber.
He tried.
They didn't want to understand.[155]

~

Death does not make me afraid.
I have loved my Love
and He will be my judge.[156]

~

No book —
no matter how beautiful or profound —
can give to my spirit
as much strength
and especially as much love
as Jesus crucified.[157]

Jesus needs people
who are capable of loving in this way:
who choose Him
not because of the joy that comes from following Him;
not because of the paradise He prepares for them
nor for some eternal reward;
and not just to feel all right.
No, no, no.
Jesus needs people
who, only because they are thirsty for true love,
want to be one with Him.[158]

⁓

Listening to his subtle voice — a Voice, a Light,
speaking to Him when He doesn't speak.
This is the life of the saint:
a love chat.[159]

When do we love you, Lord?
When have we found You?
When is it that we can be certain that we have You?
When we trust only in You
and madly turn our eyes towards Heaven,
and when we seek only You:
our Father,
God.[160]

~

If you ask, you do not have.
If you give, you will have.
If you want to ask something of God's fullness,
ask to "give."
"Grant me to love You,
Lord,
with immense love,
love as immense as your Heart."[161]

Let us allow our hearts
only one need:
the need to love!
Let us allow our minds
only one need:
constantly to confront every thought
with the abundant and endless
love of God.[162]

Wise is the one
who dies,
so as to let God
live in her.[163]

I feel my powerlessness,
but I abandon it to God.
I base everything
on a faith that won't crumble,
I believe in the love of God.
I believe that God loves me.
And because of this love
I ask great things from my life
and from the lives of those who walk in my ideal,
things worthy of people who know that they are loved by one who is God.[164]

∼

Always remain faithful to Him
and inherit from my heart
the only treasure I have:
the infinite desire
to love Him
as no one
has ever loved Him before![165]

Since God descended from Heaven
and came on earth for us,
there can be no doubt that He loves us.
And when someone loves us,
even more, when God Himself loves us,
everything is easier for us on earth,
easier to understand.
Beyond life's dark lines
we discern His loving hand at work,
a reason for things often goes unnoticed
   by us,
a loving reason.
Everything becomes more bearable then,
more pervaded throughout with joy,
if we are already dealing in joy.
Because beyond life's sweet brushstrokes —
a beautiful love that blossoms,
the birth of a child,
a sudden fortune —
there is the presence of the Father's
   Providence.

Then everything becomes possible.
If you believe, if you believe in a God
    who loves us,
every impossibility is shattered,
even the seemingly apparent
    impossibility
that this cradle, our planet, which is our
    home
can be at peace.
Yes, everything is possible.
Indeed, since the Almighty has come
    among us,
our faith can reach even further.
We can believe that if we hope and ask
    with all our heart,
our world can move toward unity:
to harmony between social classes,
between races,
between Christians divided for centuries,
between believers of different religions,
between peoples of every nation.[166]

Notes

These texts belong to the archives of the Chiara Lubich Center, via della Madonnella 10, 00040 Rocca di Papa, Rome, Italy.

[1] Letter of April 1945.
[2] Writing from the 1940's.
[3] Letter of Easter 1945.
[4] Letter of Easter 1945.
[5] Letter of 8 September 1948.
[6] Letter of 1943.
[7] Letter of 1943.
[8] Letter of August 1945.
[9] Letter from after Easter 1945.
[10] Letter of 6 November 1947.
[11] Writing of 12 December 1946.
[12] Letter of June 1944.
[13] Writing, February 1948.
[14] Letter of 1 November 1947.
[15] Letter of August 1945.
[16] Letter of 1943.
[17] Letter of 7 June 1944.
[18] Letter of August 1945.
[19] Letter of 1943.
[20] Letter, 1 November 1947.
[21] Letter of 1944.
[22] Letter of 8 September 1948.
[23] Writing from the 1940's.
[24] Letter of the 1940's.
[25] Letter of the 1940's.
[26] Diary, 13 January 1979.
[27] Letter of 3 September 1947.
[28] Letter of 8 September 1948.
[29] Letter of 23 April 1948.
[30] Letter of the 1940's.
[31] Letter of the 1940's.
[32] Letter of 8 December 1944.
[33] Letter of 27 January 1946.
[34] Letter of 1 June 1945.
[35] Letter, Advent 1944.
[36] Writing of August 1949.
[37] Writing of 2 December 1946.
[38] Letter of the 1940's.
[39] Writing of 26 June 1949.
[40] Letter of 8 September 1949.
[41] Letter of June 1944.
[42] Letter of June 1944.
[43] Letter of 8 September 1948.
[44] Letter of Christmas 1944.
[45] Letter of 4 November 1948.
[46] Writing of 1 – 2 June 1958.
[47] Letter of 14 August 1948.
[48] Letter of the 1940's.
[49] Letter of the 1940's.
[50] Letter of the 1940's.
[51] Letter of August 1945.
[52] Letter of 11 May 1948.
[53] Letter of June 1944.
[54] Letter of 23 April 1948.
[55] Letter of 7 June 1944.
[56] Letter of 1 January 1949 (for the New Year).
[57] Letter of 24 September 1948.

[58] Writing of 25 May 2000.
[59] Letter of 23 April 1948.
[60] Writing from the 1940's.
[61] Letter of 15 June 1948.
[62] Letter of 1 June 1945.
[63] Letter of 1 November 1947.
[64] Letter of 13 November 1947.
[65] Letter of 1943.
[66] Letter of 27 January 1946.
[67] Letter of 15 June 1948.
[68] Letter of 29 June 1945.
[69] Letter of Easter 1945.
[70] Letter of the 1940's.
[71] Letter of December 1944.
[72] Letter of the 1940's.
[73] Letter of the 1940's.
[74] From *Detti Gen*, Città Nuova, Rome 1999.
[75] From *Detti Gen*, Città Nuova, Rome 1999.
[76] Letter of 6 November 1947.
[77] Letter of 1 June 1945.
[78] Letter of 11 January 1945.
[79] Letter of the 1940's.
[80] Writing of 1 January 1945.
[81] Letter of 29 April 1948.
[82] Letter of 16 April 1944.
[83] Letter of the 1940's.
[84] Letter of August 1945.
[85] Letter of the 1940's.
[86] Letter of June 1944.
[87] Writing of 2 December 1946.
[88] Letter of June 1943.
[89] Letter of 6 September 1947.
[90] Letter of 6 August 1947.
[91] Letter of the 1940's.
[92] Letter of 7 June 1944.
[93] Letter of August 1945.
[94] Writing from the 1940's.
[95] Letter of 1 April 1948.
[96] From *Detti Gen*, Città Nuova, Rome 1999.
[97] Letter of Easter 1945.
[98] Letter of June 1944.
[99] Letter of 1949.
[100] Letter of 11 May 1948.
[101] Letter, June 1949.
[102] Writing of 1947.
[103] Letter of the 1940's.
[104] Letter of 1 November 1947.
[105] Letter of the 1940's.
[106] Letter of the 1940's.
[107] Letter of 15 June 1948.
[108] Letter of the 1940's.
[109] Letter of 1 June 1945
[110] Letter of 1 January 1945.
[111] Writing of September 1947.
[112] Writing of September 1947.
[113] Letter of the 1940's.
[114] Writing of September 1947.
[115] Writing of September 1947.
[116] Letter of the 1940's.
[117] Letter of the 1940's.
[118] Letter of the 1940's.
[119] Letter, June 1949.
[120] Writing of 14 January 1988.
[121] Letter of 3 October 1946.
[122] Writing of 2 December 1946.
[123] Writing of 2 June 1945.
[124] Letter of the 1940's.
[125] Writing of September 1947.
[126] Letter of 10 March 1944.
[127] Letter of the 1940's.
[128] Letter of 1 June 1945.

[129] Writing of September 1947.
[130] Letter of 16 April 1944.
[131] Letter of the 1940's.
[132] Letter of 20 August 1949.
[133] Letter of Eastertide 1945.
[134] Letter of June 1944.
[135] Letter of the 1940's.
[136] Writing of 24 October 1949.
[137] Writing of June 1947.
[138] Letter of 5 September 1948.
[139] Writing of 2 December 1946.
[140] Letter of 3 October 1946.
[141] Letter of 1 April 1948.
[142] Letter of 5 September 1948.
[143] Letter of 6 August 1949.
[144] Letter, June 1949.
[145] Letter of 15 June 1948.
[146] Letter of June 1949.
[147] Letter of 5 September 1948.
[148] Letter of 27 January 1945.
[149] Letter of 11 May 1948.
[150] Letter of 1943.
[151] Letter of 16 April 1944.
[152] Writing of September 1947.
[153] Writing of 2 December 1946.
[154] Writing of October 1948.
[155] Writing of March 1947.
[156] Letter of 9 June 1945.
[157] Letter of 7 June 1944.
[158] Letter of 5 January 1947.
[159] Letter of 14 October 1946.
[160] Letter of 14 October 1946.
[161] Letter of 1943.
[162] Letter of June 1944.
[163] Letter of 29 April 1948.
[164] Letter of 16 April 1944.
[165] Letter of 9 January 1945.
[166] Writing of Christmas 1985.

Since the texts collected in this anthology are mostly from personal letters written by Chiara Lubich to several recipients, it was necessary to make some slight adjustments to the original texts to ensure the proper understanding outside of the context in which they were composed.

For Further Reading

Marisa Cerini, *God Who Is Love in the Experience and Thought of Chiara Lubich* (Hyde Park, NY: New City Press, 1992).

Chiara Lubich, *Essential Writings: Spirituality, Dialogue, Culture* (Hyde Park, NY: New City Press, 2007), 55–65.

Chiara Lubich, *A New Way: The Spirituality of Unity* (Hyde Park, NY: New City Press, 2006), 37–41.